# Honouring My Wishes: Me & Mine

**Evelyn48**

BLUEROSE PUBLISHERS
India | U.K.

Copyright © Evelyn48 2024

All rights reserved by author. No part of this publication may be reproduced, stored in a retrieval system or transmitted in any form or by any means, electronic, mechanical, photocopying, recording or otherwise, without the prior permission of the author. Although every precaution has been taken to verify the accuracy of the information contained herein, the publisher assumes no responsibility for any errors or omissions. No liability is assumed for damages that may result from the use of information contained within.

BlueRose Publishers takes no responsibility for any damages, losses, or liabilities that may arise from the use or misuse of the information, products, or services provided in this publication.

For permissions requests or inquiries regarding this publication, please contact:

BLUEROSE PUBLISHERS
www.BlueRoseONE.com
info@bluerosepublishers.com
+91 8882 898 898
+4407342408967

ISBN: 978-1-7399266-7-0

First Edition: September 2024

*Evelyn 48*

**The Finale Full Stop**

*Evelyn 48*

# Content

# Content

» Family Documents

» Child/Children/Grand-Child Children/Guardianship

» Medical Information (blank page)

» Pets

*Evelyn 48*

# Acknowledgement

I would like to thank my family, loved ones and friends who helped me along the journey of developing the brand Evelyn48 and Honouring My Wishes Me and Mine

I thank God for the inspiration placed upon me daily.

Thank you to my sister Patricia St. Hilaire and our cousin Sharon Forbes who both listened to me and repeatedly read and commented on numerous drafts.

Thank you, Satwinder Kundhi (NiQi), my design consultant from Print Inn

Thank you to Michael Francis, my partner who joined me on the journey of Evelyn48 taking the time to understand my dream. Thank you for building relationships and creating interest in Evelyn48 in the North of England while supporting me and developing the Evelyn48 App.

To Deirdre Coward, my dearest friend from way back, who listened to me as we drove to and from our nights out, I say "Thank you."

Thank you, Abi Carter of African Caribbean Funeral Homes.

Thank you to Maxine Edgar of Bronze Ash Funerals.

Thank you to the focus groups for all the encouragement, thoughtful insights and suggestions.

Jackee Holder, Yinka Bandele, Mark Johnson, Sophia Powell, Maudlyn Aaron, Antonio Stewart

Thank you to my 5 mentors who joined my journey at different times and the procrastination clubs I paid to attend that held me accountable.

Last but not least, I thank my mother, Evelyn who lived at number 48. I set out to find a way to honour and remember my mum, at a granular level. Thank you Mummy xx

# Introduction

*Dear Friends and Family,*

Life is full of complexities, uncertainties, and countless choices. I wanted to share some important information as I prepare for the future, especially regarding my children and grandchildren.

As you know, I've been working on documenting my wishes and support for them in case something unexpected happens. This book, "Me and Mine," captures essential details about our family dynamics, aspirations, and what matters most to us.

While this book may not cover every detail, it provides a roadmap to navigate through important decisions.

Thinking about these matters can be overwhelming, but I believe in planning ahead. Your support and understanding mean a lot to me.

Together, we can ensure that my wishes are honoured and our family's future is safeguarded.

Thank you all for your love and care.

*Warm regards*

# Owner

**Name:** _____

**Address:** _____

**Phone:** _____

**Email:** _____

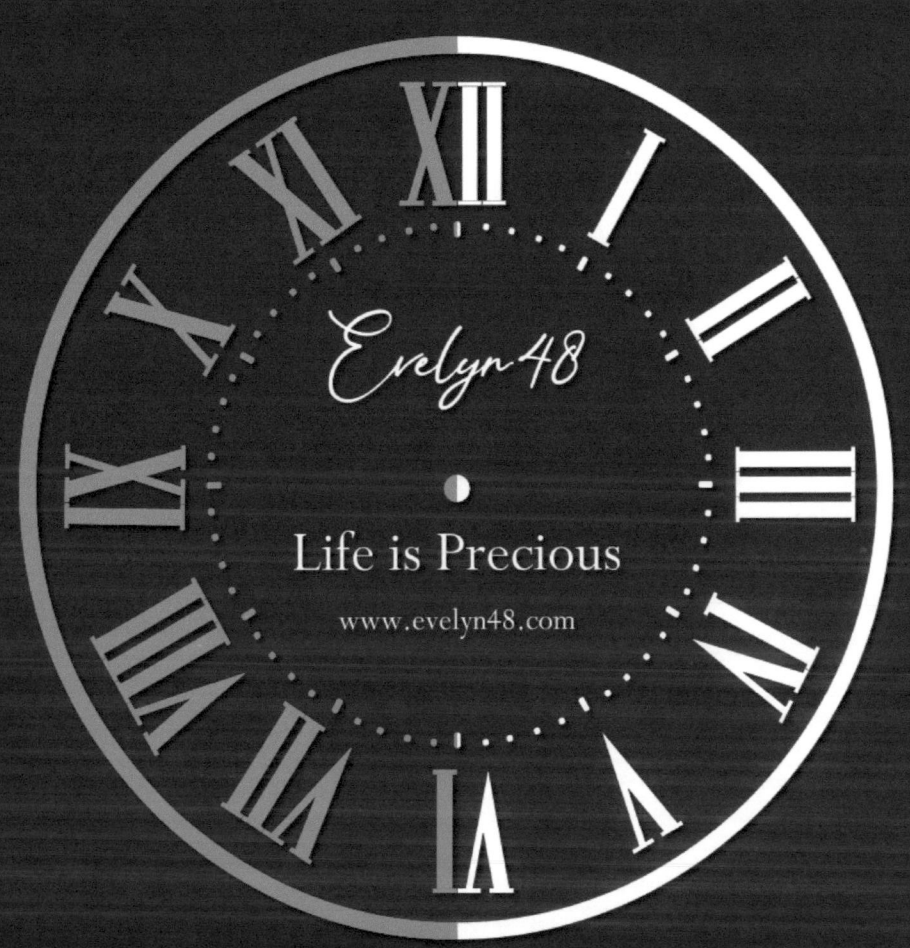

**Official Name:** _____

**Maiden Name:** _____

**Nick Name:** _____

**Gender:** _____

**Address:** _____

**Place of Birth (City)** _____

# Family Documents

# Family Documents

| Document Type | Document Number | Issue Date | Expiry Date |
|---|---|---|---|
| Marriage Licence/Certificate. | | | |
| Divorce Papers. | | | |
| Deed Poll Documents. | | | |
| Birth Certificate. | | | |
| Children's Birth Certificate(s) | | | |
| Passport Number. | | | |
| National Insurance Number. | | | |
| Driver Licence (add copy). | | | |
| Copies in the folder | | | |

# Child/Children/Grand-Child Children/Guardianship

*Child/Children/Grand-Child Children/Guardianship*

## *Dear Friends and Family,*

Life is full of complexities, uncertainties, and countless choices. I wanted to share some important information as I prepare for the future, especially regarding my children and grandchildren.

As you know, I've been working on documenting my wishes and support for them in case something unexpected happens. This book, "Me and Mine," captures essential details about our family dynamics, aspirations, and what matters most to us.

While this book may not cover every detail, it provides a roadmap to navigate through important decisions.

Thinking about these matters can be overwhelming, but I believe in planning ahead. Your support and understanding mean a lot to me.

Together, we can ensure that my wishes are honoured and our family's future is safeguarded.

Thank you all for your love and care.

***Warm regards***

# Child/Children/Grand-Child Children/Guardianship

| Child One | |
|---|---|
| Full Name: | |
| Address: | |
| Town/City: | |
| County: | |
| Postal Code: | |
| E-mail Address: | |
| Telephone number: | |

| Child Two | |
|---|---|
| Full Name: | |
| Address: | |
| Town/City: | |
| County: | |
| Postal Code: | |
| E-mail Address: | |
| Telephone number: | |

# Child/Children/Grand-Child Children/Guardianship

| Child Three | |
|---|---|
| Full Name: | |
| Address: | |
| Town/City: | |
| County: | |
| Postal Code: | |
| E-mail Address: | |
| Telephone number: | |

| Child Four | |
|---|---|
| Full Name: | |
| Address: | |
| Town/City: | |
| County: | |
| Postal Code: | |
| E-mail Address: | |
| Telephone number: | |

# Child/Children/Grand-Child Children/Guardianship

| Child Five | |
|---|---|
| Full Name: | |
| Address: | |
| Town/City: | |
| County: | |
| Postal Code: | |
| E-mail Address: | |
| Telephone number: | |

| Child Six | |
|---|---|
| Full Name: | |
| Address: | |
| Town/City: | |
| County: | |
| Postal Code: | |
| E-mail Address: | |
| Telephone number: | |

# Child/Children/Grand-Child Children/Guardianship

| Guardian One | |
|---|---|
| Full Name: | |
| Address: | |
| Town/City: | |
| County: | |
| Postal Code: | |
| E-mail Address: | |
| Telephone number: | |

| Guardian Two | |
|---|---|
| Full Name: | |
| Address: | |
| Town/City: | |
| County: | |
| Postal Code: | |
| E-mail Address: | |
| Telephone number: | |

# Child/Children/Grand-Child Children/Guardianship

| Guardian Three | |
|---|---|
| Full Name: | |
| Address: | |
| Town/City: | |
| County: | |
| Postal Code: | |
| E-mail Address: | |
| Telephone number: | |

| Guardian Four | |
|---|---|
| Full Name: | |
| Address: | |
| Town/City: | |
| County: | |
| Postal Code: | |
| E-mail Address: | |
| Telephone number: | |

| | |
|---|---|
| What relation are the guardian to the child/children/Grand-Child (if any)? | |
| Have you left any written instructions for the guardians of your child/children/ Grand-Child as to your preferences in any of the topics raised earlier in this section? (education/ religion etc.). If so, where are these instructions? | |
| For the sake of completeness, it is worth clarifying a few details. Please write the names of your child/children/Grand-Child and their dates of birth. | |
| If your child/children/Grand-Child are still living at home, please note where birth certificates, medical details and passports are kept. | |
| Are there any special requests (regarding your child/children/ Grand-Child) that aren't in your Will which you wish to address now? | |

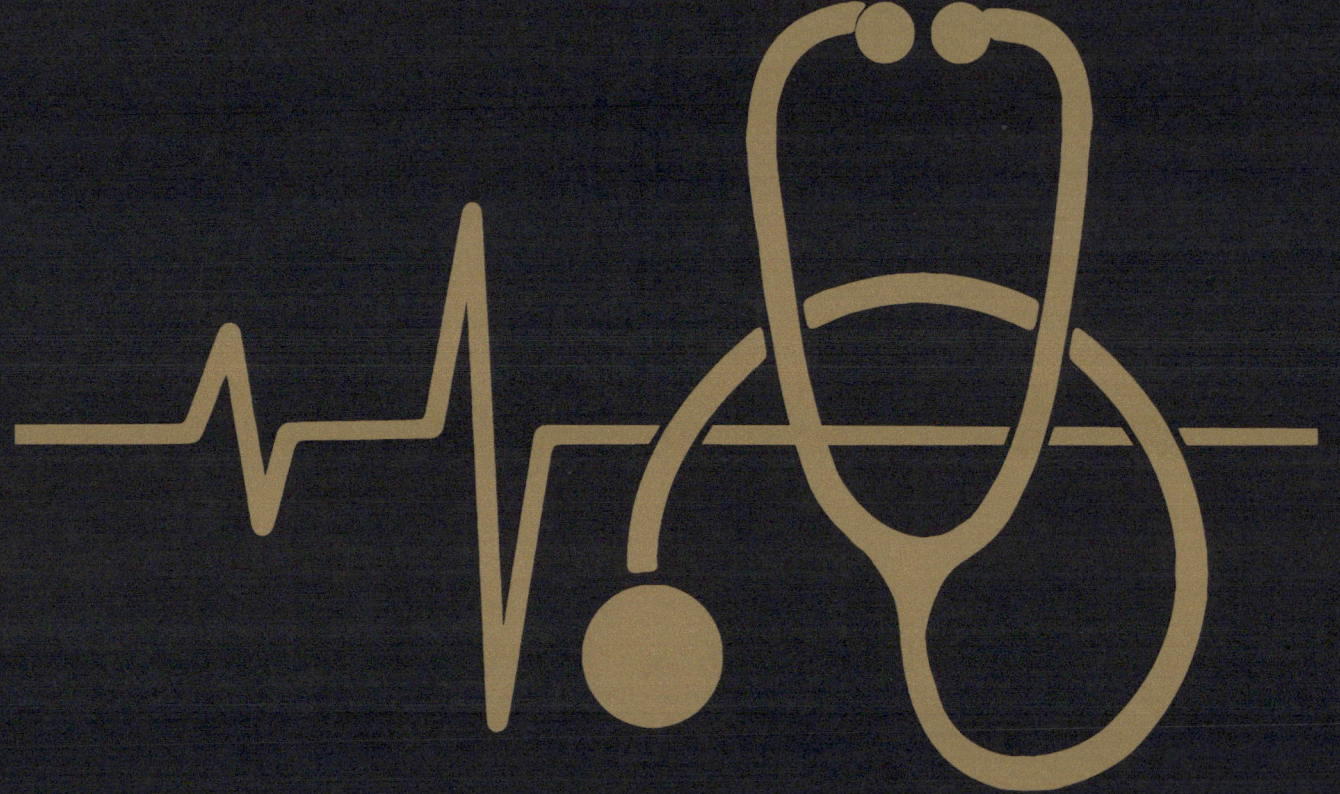

# Medical Information

# Medical Information

| | |
|---|---|
| **Height** | |
| **Weight** | |
| **Distinguishing Marks** | |
| ⦿ Tattoos | |
| ⦿ Birthmarks | |
| **Adornments** | |
| ⦿ Permanent | |
| ⦿ Temporary | |
| ⦿ Prosthetics | |
| **Implants** | |
| **Surgical Operations** | |
| **Dental Implants** | |

| | | | |
|---|---|---|---|
| General Practitioner: | | HEALTH INSURANCE | |
| Address: | | Company Name: | |
| | | Reference Number: | |
| Town/City: | | Telephone Number: | |
| Postal Code: | | Website: | |
| Telephone Number: | | Payment Amount: | |
| Email Address: | | Payment Account: | |
| NHS Number: | | Payment Date: | |
| Dentist: | | | |
| Address: | | Prepaid Prescription | |
| | | Payment Amount: | |
| Town/City: | | Payment Account: | |
| Postal Code: | | Payment Date: | |
| Telephone Number: | | Travel Insurance | |
| Email Address: | | Company Name | |
| | | Policy Number | |

| | |
|---|---|
| Are you registered as an organ donor? | |
| Or do you carry a donor card? | |
| Where is it? | |
| Have you made a Living Will? | |
| Where is the paperwork to support this? | |
| Who knows about this? | |
| Have you signed a Power of Attorney? | |
| If so, where is the paperwork for this? | |
| Who knows about this? | |
| Please share details of any historic family illnesses. Be sure to include your health and that of your parents and grandparents. What ages did they pass away, and what was the cause of death? These can help loved ones keep track of the family's health history. | |

# Pets

# Pets

Do you have a pet? Someone will need to take care of them. Whilst anyone close may know the pet's name, few will know about the day-to-day care that your pet is used to, so completing this section will be very helpful. If you have more than one pet, complete the answers below in different coloured pens or symbols for each pet. Alternatively, having a folder specifically relating to each pet may be helpful.

| | |
|---|---|
| What is your pet's name, breed and date of birth? | |
| If your pet is a pedigree, do you have the documentation to support this? You may include details of the breeder. | |
| Is there anyone you would like to look after your pet(s)? | |
| Equally important, is there anyone who you would rather did not take care of your pet(s)? | |
| Are there any special instructions which are needed for the care of the pet? | |

| | |
|---|---|
| What type of food does your pet(s) eat? | |
| Does your pet have any special dietary needs? | |
| Does your pet(s) have any vaccination certificates? | |
| Does your pet(s) have any medical condition(s)? | |
| Does your pet attend a particular veterinary practice? | |
| Please supply details of the name and address of the vet. | |
| Is your pet covered by any form of insurance (in respect of vet's fees?) please leave documentation with other policies in your files. | |
| Which kennel/cattery does your pet(s) normally go to? | |
| Is your pet(s) micro-chipped? Where is the documentation to support this? | |
| Have you assembled a file about your pet(s)? If so, where is it kept? | |

*A Personal Note*

# A Personal Note

# A Personal Note

*A Personal Note*

www.ingramcontent.com/pod-product-compliance
Lightning Source LLC
Chambersburg PA
CBHW041649160426

43209CB00020B/1864